The Garrison of Québec from 1748 to 1759

Gilles Proulx

Translated from the original French

Studies in Archaeology, Architecture and History

National Historic Sites
Parks Service
Environment Canada

©Minister of Supply and Services Canada 1991.

Available in Canada through authorized bookstore agents and other bookstores, or by mail from Canada Communication Group - Publishing, Supply and Services Canada, Ottawa, Ontario, Canada, K1A 0S9.

Published under the authorization
of the Minister of the Environment,
Ottawa, 1991.

Editing: Sheila Ascroft
Design: Suzanne Adam-Filion
Desktop production: Suzanne H. Rochette
Translation: Secretary of State
Cover: Soldier on sentry duty at the St. Louis Gate. Illustration by Francis Back. Parks Service, Environment Canada.

Parks publishes the results of its research in archaeology, architecture and history. A list of our publications is available from National Historic Sites Publications, Parks Service, Environment Canada, 1600 Liverpool Court, Ottawa, K1A 0H3.

Canadian Cataloguing in Publication Data

Proulx, Gilles

The Garrison of Québec from 1748 to 1759

(Studies in archaeology, architecture and history,
ISSN 0821-1027)
Issued also in French under title: La garnison de Québec de 1748 à 1759
Includes bibliographical references.
ISBN 0-660-14276-7
DSS cat. no. R61-2/9-55E

1. Garrisons – Quebec (Province) – Quebec – History – 18th century.
2. Soldiers – Quebec (Province) – Quebec – Social life and customs.
3. Quebec (Quebec) – History. I. Canadian Parks Service. National Historic Sites. II. Title. III. Series.

U375.C32P7613 1991   971.4'471014   C92-099511-X

Table of Contents

Introduction 5

Organization and Management of Military Forces 13

Background of the Military 17

Soldiers and their Environment 25

Military Activities 41

Living Habits and Leisure Activities 49

Conclusion 53

Bibliographic Note 55

Submitted for publication by Gilles Proulx, Historian, Quebec Regional Office, Parks Service, Environment Canada.

Introduction

The city of Québec was the nerve centre of the entire French colonial administration in Canada, from the founding of New
France in 1608 until 1760. As capital of the colony, Québec was
the seat of the government and, in an era when the army was the
right arm of the political power, required a military presence to
uphold its authority. As the major port of the colony, Québec
was in even greater need of soldiers, to control colonial imports
and exports and to defend its facilities. Throughout its history,
New France and its government had to contend with two persist-
ent adversaries, the Amerindians and the English. Battles were
always being fought, and between 1608 and 1760 there were
barely 50 years when the people experienced even relatively
peaceful conditions.

In the 17th century, the government and settlers of New
France formed various alliances in an attempt to exploit potential rivalries among Amerindian tribes to their own advantage.
The goal of these new arrivals was to establish the economic
foundations of New France by expanding their access to furs,
the easiest form of wealth for them to acquire. Such machina-
tions, however, led inevitably to more or less serious reprisals
on the part of the Amerindians. Furthermore, by the end of the
17th century, France and England were extending their Euro-
pean rivalry to America, a practice that was to continue until
1760. Each country wanted to increase its economic power by
dominating or containing the colonial expansion of the other.
While the French were trying to keep the English in their settle-
ments on the Atlantic coast, the English became aware of how

valuable the land was that the French were acquiring in the northern and central regions of America. The leaders of New France and Québec soon found that they had to rely on soldiers to assert their claims against the Amerindians and the English. Who were these soldiers who defended New France, and what kind of life did they lead through all these conflicts?

New France was founded by Champlain in 1608, but had no professional soldiers - men paid to bear arms - until 1632. The first shots fired in Québec came from civilians anxious to preserve their interests, and when New France had to be defended civilians were always in the forefront. This civilian contribution to the defence of New France was formalized in 1669, when Governor De Courcelle organized militia companies. All able-bodied males between the ages of 16 and 60 not employed in the civil service were required to enrol in these companies and to serve when necessary. Occasionally, the men were also called upon to perform transportation duties or to work on military facilities.

Each parish and, in the towns and cities, each district had its own militia company. For example, in 1754 the city of Québec had 14 companies. The number of soldiers varied according to the size of the parish or district. The men supplied their own equipment, served on expeditions without pay and took part in arms-training exercises once a month. Each company was commanded by a captain, who was also the government representative in the parish. This militia organization provided New France with an armed citizenry accustomed to waging war. Even though members of the militia did not have to serve in garrisons, all the measures adopted in connection with this system helped to make the colony easier to defend and increased its security. In addition to the militia companies of civilians, there were three other kinds of military organizations which, successively and sometimes jointly, ensured the defence of New France.

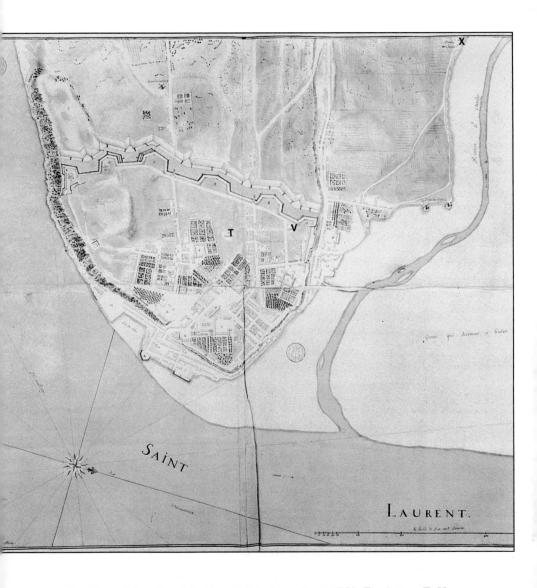

1 Plan of the city of Quebec dating from about 1750. The letters T, V
   and X indicate the buildings that were to become barracks. *France.*
   Archives nationales, Dépôt des fortifications et des colonies, 436.

During the period 1632-65 two commercial enterprises, the Company of One Hundred Associates and the Habitants' Company, hired soldiers to serve in Canada and paid for their maintenance. There were rarely more than 100 soldiers at any given time, the garrison of Québec had fewer than 20 men, and these served mainly in the Château Saint-Louis. Almost no information is available on the lives of these men before they came to Canada or on the services they rendered after they arrived. They do not appear to have been organized along strict hierarchical lines, since there is no mention of commissioned officers but only of non-commissioned ranks, such as sergeants and corporals. The soldiers hired by these companies were more concerned with protecting members of the government than with defending the country, a task left mainly to the settlers. The limited number of soldiers and perhaps the poor quality of their services may very well explain why by 1661-62, despite a short respite in the wars brought about by the exploits of Dollard des Ormeaux, New France was on the verge of panic in the face of the Iroquois threat.

In 1663 Louis XIV took the administration of New France firmly in hand by implementing a few strong measures designed to defend the colony. Between 1665-68, 1200 hundred men, members of the Carignan regiment and of four companies drawn from the Chambellé, Lallier, Orléans and Poitou regiments, were sent to Canada. The Ministry of War sent 24 companies of 50 men each to fight the Iroquois and to allay the fears of the *Canadiens*. These actions were obviously effective, since two expeditions without battle and the construction of several forts along the Richelieu were enough to dissuade the Iroquois from further fighting and to bring about a peace that lasted for approximately 15 years. In 1668 these infantry troops returned to France, leaving behind 400 men who were demobilized and allowed to settle the country. The following year, when the militia companies were being organized, six captains of the Carignan regiment returned to Canada with six companies of 50 men each. These soldiers, along with the men of the militia, constituted the country's defence forces until 1683. In 1675, for example, the garrison of Québec included 25 soldiers and two sergeants. However, the soldiers gradually abandoned the army to become settlers and, eventually, the colony was left once again without a military organization to defend it.

Not until 1755 did the Ministry of War send more of its regular forces to Canada. Eight battalions came, six drawn from the Reine, Languedoc, Béarn, Guyenne, La Sarre and Royal-Roussillon regiments and two from the Berri regiment. All in all, about 4000 men arrived during the period 1755-57, at a time when the deterioration of international relations and the demographic imbalance between the English and French colonies were raising serious doubts about the ability of New France to survive. In this same period, four other battalions, composed of men from the Artois, Burgundy, Cambis and Foreign Volunteers regiments, were sent to Louisbourg. Like their predecessors from the Carignan regiment, these members of the regular army *(troupes de terre)* did not serve in the garrison of Québec. Since some of their battalions had winter quarters in the city, however, they did have an influence on garrison life.

To fill the void in the interval between the War Ministry's two major troop shipments, another army corps was permanently assigned to New France. The new troops came under the control of the Ministry of the Navy, which in the home government was responsible for the colonies. Traditionally, these marines served in the ports of France and on the king's ships, but because of politics some of them were sent to the colonies. In 1680 there had been a resumption of hostilities with the Iroquois, and by the beginning of 1683 it was imperative to send troops to Canada. Due to differences of opinion between the Minister of War and the Minister of the Navy, the latter was obliged to send detachments of his forces to Canada. In the period 1683-88, more than 2000 of his troops, organized into 35 companies of approximately 50 men each, made the crossing to Canada. The companies were chronically understrength due to

2 Soldier of the *Compagnies franches de la Marine*, circa 1755.
  Drawing: Eugène Lelièpvre. Parks Service, Environment Canada.

deaths and desertions, and by 1689 the average company had only 28 men.

While the troops sent to the colony were clearly different from those serving in the home ports and ships, both categories were known as the *Compagnies franches de la Marine*. These companies were free of regimental organization and thus independent of one another. During the period 1690-1750, 28 of these companies were stationed in Canada. Officially, the number of men in each company remained constant at 28 to 30 for the entire period, but in reality the companies were never up to full strength. For example, the annual recruitment rate of 25 to 75 in the period 1720-45 never made up for all the voluntary and other departures that took place each year, although it did ensure an almost complete turnover of personnel every 10 years. Full strength or not, these forces were never enough to guard all the posts and garrisons in the towns of New France. Indeed, soldiers for the garrison of Québec were recruited from among the *Compagnies franches de la Marine*. During the period 1700-50, at least seven companies remained on permanent duty in the city, and after 1750 the number doubled. In the following pages, we will attempt to describe what life was like for the men who served in the garrison of Québec.

Organization and Management of Military Forces

During the period 1748-59, a garrison made up of 169 soldiers in 1748, 429 in 1751 and about 540 in 1757, provided security throughout the city of Québec and stood watch on its ramparts. In 1748 the men were recruited from seven *Compagnies franches*, and by 1750, 13 companies were contributing soldiers to the garrison. Also in 1750, an artillery company was created and added to the Québec garrison to ensure artillery service. The military forces of New France comprised 30 companies of 50 men each in 1750 and 40 companies of 65 men each in 1757. In 1751 and 1757, however, the garrison of Québec was only at about 60 percent of its full strength. While dismissals, deaths and desertions did contribute to this shortage, it was mainly brought about by the formation of detachments to serve in various posts throughout the colony.

For administrative reasons, the 30 or 40 companies serving in Canada were divided among three garrisons stationed in Québec, Trois-Rivières and Montréal. The area which the soldiers were required to defend, however, extended well beyond the Laurentian Valley to the entire Canadian hinterland, from the Richelieu Valley through the Great Lakes region all the way to the Ohio Valley. It therefore became necessary to organize detachments from the three garrisons, and their strength was diminished accordingly. For its part, the fortress of Louisbourg was defended by 24 *Compagnies franches* of 50 men each. In Louisiana, the number of companies went from 13 to 37 in 1750. Both the Louisbourg and Louisiana corps were to all intents and purposes independent of the group serving in Canada.

This scattering of soldiers throughout the colony led to serious discipline problems. Authority was undermined because officers were not always able to follow their men when they were sent on assignments. A similar situation arose with regard to the regular rotation of companies among the three Canadian garrisons and sometimes the Louisbourg garrison as well. The purpose of moving troops around was to break the monotony of routine and to rid soldiers of their bad habits by obliging them to keep changing their living quarters. However, officers often had families and properties in certain jurisdictions and sometimes refused to follow their companies, thus losing much of their control over their men. No doubt these and other circumstances explain why, in the summer of 1754, seven companies in the garrison of Québec had no officers to lead them.

At the head of each company were four officers: a captain, a lieutenant, a first ensign *(enseigne en pied)* and a second ensign *(enseigne en second)*. Companies in New France were normally identified by the name of their captain, but in 1757 ten new companies were created and given their own individual identification numbers. Each company also had five non-commissioned positions, assigned to two sergeants and three corporals. Other ranks included privates, two cadets and two drummers. Of these, only the cadets could aspire to be officers; the others could rise no higher than the rank of sergeant. The garrison of Québec also had a sergeant-major, a fifer and a drum-major. Officers were responsible for the general good conduct of their companies, while non-commissioned officers looked after the daily administrative details.

All soldiers, from privates to captains, took their orders from staff headquarters. This headquarters organization, a feature of every government in New France, was composed of the Governor, the King's lieutenant and a junior adjutant *(aide-major de place)*. At Québec only, this group also included an adjutant *(major)*. The Governor was responsible for broad general administration. The men who successively acted in this capacity from

1748 to 1759, namely La Gallisonnière, La Jonquière, Duquesne and Vaudreuil, had little direct or personal contact with the soldiers. The King's lieutenants, Pierre Joseph Lemoyne de Longueuil (1749-57) and Jean-Baptiste Nicolas de Ramesay (1758-60), did not intervene in military affairs except as replacements for the Governor. The closest contact governors and lieutenants had with individual soldiers occurred at courts-martial. On these occasions, they rendered a verdict in the company of officers, for the most part captains. Such verdicts were based on the conclusions of the prosecutor, who would have been either the adjutant or the junior adjutant.

Troop discipline was the primary responsibility of the adjutant, a position that De Ramesay held from 1749 to 1758. The adjutant also supervised officers who were part of the same garrison. The junior adjutant assisted the adjutant and had the added responsibility of ensuring supplies for the men in the garrison. The junior adjutant of Québec from 1745 to 1760 was Jean-Michel Hugues Péan. Although the Intendant François Bigot and Controller of the Navy Michel Bréard, had no authority in military affairs, they had to deal with all practical matters such as provisions, accommodation, equipment and identifications for all soldiers stationed in Canada, some of whom lived in Québec for fairly long periods of time.

Background of the Military

To become a member of the *Compagnies franches de la Marine* or of the regular army (*troupes de terre*), a man had to be at least 16 years old and five feet five inches tall, and had to enlist for a six-year term of duty. In return, recruits received an enlistment bonus from the King of 30 *livres*. These terms were prescribed by the Military Code. However, we know from identification records inventoried by researchers into the military of New France and of Québec in particular, that many soldiers in the *Compagnies franches* did not satisfy the minimum height requirement. Five feet five inches was actually the average height of the soldiers. On the other hand, artillerymen, who were recruited from the *Compagnies franches*, all exceeded the required standard. Since the tallest soldiers were reputed to be the best, the slightly greater height of the artillerymen gave their corps a more elitist character.

An extensive sampling of the ages of soldiers serving in Québec in the early 1750s has shown that not many were under 16. In fact, the average age was between 20 and 25, with nearly 90 percent under 31. Most of the soldiers, then, were fairly young and in their prime. The artillerymen, who were selected from among members of the *Compagnies franches*, tended to be a little older than this average. It is almost impossible to gauge exactly how long soldiers actually served or whether a number of them signed up for a second term. Considering their rather young age on the average, it is safe to assume that most soldiers did not extend their years of military service for too long. Every rule has exceptions of course. In 1752 Pierre Beauvais *dit* Lé-

3   Artillerymen working with a piece of marine artillery.
  Drawing: Eugène Lilièpvre. Company of Military Historians.

veillé, a young soldier in the Bonne company, acknowledged that he had joined the military in 1749, when he was only 13. At the opposite end of the scale, three sergeants and a corporal received discharges in 1751, all four of them having served for a period of at least 25 years. Sergeants and corporals, however, as opposed to privates, were allowed to remain in the service when they married.

More than 90 percent of the men in the *Compagnies franches* were made up of non-commissioned officers and other ranks from France, two-thirds of them being natives of the coastal provinces or of the northern part of the country. Few men from the south of France joined the ranks of the *Compagnies franches*, no doubt because the Canadian climate did not appeal to them. Proximity to the ports of embarcation for New France was as important a factor as any in the fact that most of these soldiers came from France's Atlantic coast. Men from the border provinces of France and from the Caribbean made up the remaining complement of *Compagnies franches*. *Canadiens* did not serve in the regular army because they preferred to devote their energies to farming, commerce or the fur trade, all of which paid better than military service. Moreover, the government had no interest in recruiting them because they were needed in the militia forces, which were used to respond to military emergencies. Recruitment of men from the home country to serve in the *Compagnies franches* also increased the population of the colony and its labour force, which was in rather short supply. Canada had always needed more workers, but during the building of the fortifications at Québec from 1745 to 1757, this need became much more urgent and may have been a reason for the increase, in 1750, of the number of men in each company from 30 to 50.

The King entrusted the enlistment of men for these troops to professional recruiters and to officers who wanted to bring their units up to full strength. The recruiters were undoubtedly less concerned than the officers about the aptitude for military service of their recruits, and some of their less judicious choices may account for the letters sent by Canada's colonial authorities to the home government complaining about recruits who were too old or infirm. Officers exercised more care in choosing their recruits because the effectiveness of their companies depended on the quality of their soldiers. Were men recruited by force or did they volunteer? A number of those who enlisted did not know that they were going to Canada, while others signed their names or an X on forms they often had not or could not read because they were too drunk or were illiterate. Some were profligates sent to Canada under on orders issued under the king's personal seal *(lettres de cachet)*; others were smugglers exiled from France. Most recruits, however, were trying to escape unfavorable economic conditions and enlisted for the pay and rations that went with military service. The case of François Martial Philippe typifies the recruiting procedure followed in France. Philippe, a 24-year-old Catholic wigmaker and native of Bethune in Artois (now Pas de Calais), was hired in Paris by a recruiter named Dogebré. In Paris, he passed in review before the Marquis de Brézé and, after signing up, made his way along with other recruits to Belle-Isle, where he boarded The *Catin,* a ship bound for Québec. In the course of the voyage, certain incidents occurred that led to his being brought to trial when he disembarked at Québec in late August 1750. When Philippe was cross-examined at the trial, he maintained that he had not received the 10 *écus* promised to him at the time of his enlistment. We do not know why Philippe signed up, but it seems that he had already served in the Royal Wallon regiment and therefore had some military experience.

By 1750, the officer corps of the *Compagnies franches* consisted of some 180 men, including cadets, almost all of whom had been born in Canada or had been settled there for a long time. French officers showed little interest in coming to Canada to pursue their military careers, as opportunities for promotion in the colony were too limited. In Canada as in France, commissions were reserved for an aristocracy based on blood and, occasionally, on money. Most *Canadien* officers were descended from officers who had come to Canada with the Carignan Regiment or with the first Navy troops in the late 17th century. Often, they were members of the seigneurial class as well. A military career opened up excellent prospects for young men of the *Canadian* gentry, especially when they were called upon to serve in the interior of the country where, as officers, they were able to control the fur trade in their own particular areas of operation.

According to available documentation, about half the soldiers in the *Compagnies franches* had a trade. A study of the trades identified in the records indicates that they related mainly to food, clothing and shelter, the three major concerns of the colony in its early years. Given the fairly young average age of the soldiers, they were far more likely to be apprentices than master workmen. According to the colonial authorities, the moral character of the soldiers often left much to be desired. They maintained that the men were undisciplined and that many of them were thieves and mutineers - in general, they were a bad lot. Such comments were no doubt tinged with propaganda, especially when they came from a governor who followed them up with a self-congratulatory account of how he had managed to restore discipline. Soldiers of these companies were doubtless guilty of breaking the law now and again, since this was often the only way they could put forward their claims. However, the offences they committed do not seem to have been much more numerous or serious than those committed by civilians.

The settlement of New France was governed by an austere religious approach. This policy aimed at excluding Protestant settlers, and it affected the military population in that soldiers either had to be Catholic or convert. Despite the presence of some Calvinist, Lutheran and Anglican soldiers, particularly during the Seven Years' War, there was a substantial degree of religious uniformity among members of the military. Non-Catholics were forced to recant their errors. In 1758 for example, military police conducted an investigation into the conduct of Charles Daniel Sylva, a Jew from Bayonne and a soldier in the new Sixth Company; shortly afterwards he converted to Catholicism. Occasionally the Church found very specific ways to encourage conversion, as illustrated by the case of a Calvinist soldier who received an extra half-ration for a year following his conversion, on the recommendation of the priest. Religious practice, weekly attendance at mass and participation in Easter communion were of course compulsory for all soldiers. The Recollect Fathers made sure that religious services were provided for members of the Québec garrison.

A number of signatures in the parish registers of Notre-Dame de Québec have been identified as those of soldiers, suggesting that not all members of the *Compagnie franches* in Canada were illiterate. About 40 percent of enlisted men were able to sign their names, and among non-commissioned officers the figure was 70 percent. Higher ranks thus seem, on the whole, to be somewhat better educated. Of course, a soldier might be able to sign his name without really knowing how to read and write. Probably the most striking illustration of this kind of situation is the case of Denis Lemoine, who went by the name of "the Parisian." Sent to Canada in 1752 for immoral behaviour, which in his case consisted of refusing to learn to read and write, Lemoine was still able to sign his testimony. In the course of the same proceedings, an inventory of the contents of a chest belonging to a discharged soldier by the name of Bonin included at least two books of a religious nature, an indication that the man had some basic reading skills.

The signatures in the parish registers suggest not only that some soldiers were capable of signing their names but that they were fairly accustomed to writing, since the signatures do not look as if they were simply drawn or traced out. Problems of communication were not, however, confined to the written word. Some of the soldiers who served in Canada as members of the *Compagnies franches* spoke nothing but English or German.

Interpreters were sometimes needed to explain the regulations, a situation that must surely have caused a few difficulties.

To sum up then, the typical soldier in the *Compagnies franches* was a native of northern France, rather short and fairly young, who had no doubt enlisted to escape unfavorable economic conditions at home. Once in Canada, such men served under *Canadien* officers and tried to adapt to their new environment.

Soldiers and their Environment

Although soldiers were recruited in France, they were not incorporated into the *Compagnies franches* until they had crossed the Atlantic. Once disembarked, they were usually able to spend some time in the city of Québec, depending on the company to which they were assigned. Aside from the years that saw major troop shipments requiring several sailing ships to transport all the men involved (for example, 1750 and the period 1755-58), the King's ship normally took 25 to 75 recruits a year to Canada. As a rule, the men crossed the Atlantic on a military transport ship with two decks and an armament of 50 guns. About 435 people, including a crew of 250, were jammed on a vessel that was only 140 feet long, 37 feet wide and 17.5 feet deep under the master beam. The recruits, like the sailors, slept below decks in hammocks hung from the beams of the ship. Since the separation between decks was just over five feet, soldiers and sailors had to keep their shoulders constantly hunched over in order to move around.

The voyages lasted approximately nine weeks, during which time the men gradually became accustomed to the rolling and pitching of the ship. The more difficult adjustment was learning to live in rather close quarters in so large a group. If the wind started to blow hard, the ship took on water and everything became soaked. It was impossible to open the gun ports to allow for circulation and the air below deck grew stale and polluted. If the storm took a long time to abate, the men had to eat cold food, since a fire made to cook hot dishes could, under the circumstances, get out of control. The dampness, the cold, the dis-

4 View of the city of Québec as seen from the Saint-Charles River in 1761. The new barracks were housed in the long building inside the ramparts.

Drawing: R. Short. National Archives of Canada, C-359.

agreeable odours and a diet that was often deficient in vitamins and calories all helped spread contagious diseases. When the ship arrived in Québec, the sick were taken to hospital, while the fit and able-bodied were reviewed by headquarters staff and given their assignments.

*At the very same moment I received the order of my commander, to be at the Governor General's review which was to take place the following day, November 12, at Place d'Armes, for the incorporation of the recruits into the various troop companies which were garrisoned in the city but not organized in regiments since they were irregular companies known as the Compagnies franches de la Marine. I made sure I was at the review. All the troops, 18 companies in all, were called up in three lines, and the recruits stood facing each other without arms, in two lines. The Governor arrived towards noon, accompanied by the Adjutant. I joined, by choice, the line of the two gunner companies which in that country performed the functions of grenadiers. Then the Governor and Adjutant began the inspection. The commanding officer spoke to the Governor about me, the Governor examined me, and when they were finished talking about me, he walked over to the other companies and finally to the recruits, where each captain in order of seniority, starting with the captain of the gunners, took the number of men assigned to him. The commander of the gunners selected 10 men (I was not one of them) and the other captains followed suit. After a commander chose his men, his company withdrew with its recruits. I was incorporated fifth into the second company, which was housed at the St. John Gate. The next day, we were given uniforms and armed [Translation].**

---

* Excerpt from *Voyage au Canada fait dans le nord de l'Amérique septentrionale depuis l'an 1751 à 1761.* By J.C.B. New edition. Paris, Aubier-Montaigne, 1978, p. 34.

5 Soldiers' barracks.
Illustration: Francis Back. Parks Service, Environment Canada.

6   Soldiers in a tavern.
      Illustration: Francis Back, Parks Service, Environment Canada.

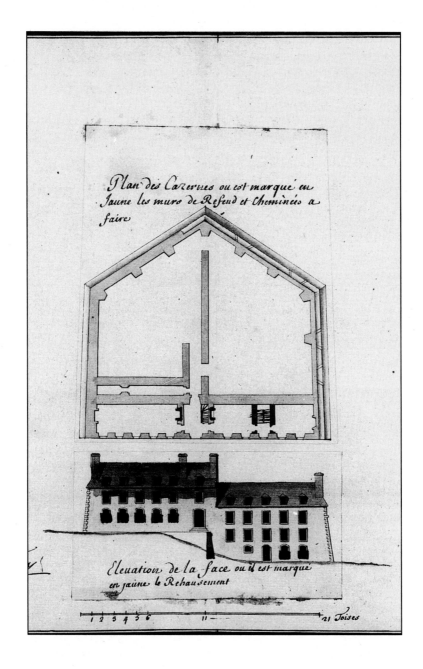

7   Plan of the Dauphine Redoubt barracks by Chaussegros de Léry.
1707. Soldiers lived in these barracks beginning in 1749.
National Archives of Canada, Ph/350.

Depending on where the government assigned them, soldiers took up service in the garrison of Québec or went to serve in other garrison towns or in border posts. One of the first tasks that had to be performed by officers of companies stationed in Québec was to find lodgings for new arrivals. Prior to 1748, soldiers were always billeted with people who lived in the city or its immediate surrounding areas. Billets on which were written the names of soldiers and their delegated hosts were given by the lieutenant-general of the Military Provost's office to the company captains, who in turn gave them to the men. *Canadiens* presented with a billet were expected to take one or two soldiers into their homes, depending on how much space they had. According to the regulations, a host was expected to supply his lodger with heat, light, a pot, a plate and a suitably outfitted bed. For his part, the lodger had to be satisfied with the room and bed provided and could not dislodge his host from his own bedroom.

Soldiers received a daily ration from the King's stores which they often turned over to their hosts. In return, they enjoyed home cooking without having to prepare their own meals. The relationships between soldiers and hosts appear to have been quite cordial. While there were certainly some instances of thefts committed by soldiers or the occasional quarrel between the parties, the lieutenant-general could move a soldier to other lodgings if his host complained. Such action appears to have been, according to the documentation presently available to us, exceedingly rare. As far as their hosts were concerned, the soldiers represented an easily accessible and very useful source of labour, especially when the soldiers let it be known that they had a talent for clearing land or were skilled in a trade. As for the soldiers, living with private individuals had a threefold advantage - home cooking, extra money from outside jobs to add to their army pay and above all, almost complete freedom of movement, since it was impossible to apply strict discipline to soldiers who were scattered across the city and suburbs of Québec.

The desire to limit this freedom and institute more effective military discipline was obviously behind the decision of the authorities to begin quartering the soldiers of Québec in barracks in 1748. At the time, Québec was the only city in Canada to have barracks. Although built much earlier, they were not used to house soldiers until 1748 because the Québec garrison had too few soldiers at first to justify the high costs involved in quartering them in barracks. It was probably easier to get people to agree to lodge soldiers in their homes than to pay more taxes to maintain the barracks. Moreover, the military custom of housing men in barracks was relatively new since it was only introduced in France when Louis XIV first came to the throne. It had been relatively easy to lodge the soldiers with civilians, so it was understandable that people might not be in favour of the barracks system. Soldiers of the *Compagnies franches* moved into the Royal Redoubt barracks in 1748 and into the Dauphine barracks in 1749. With the increase in 1750 of the number of troops coming to Canada, it became necessary to build more barracks. To house the soldiers in the meantime, the government rented houses in the Lower Town. Construction of the New Barracks, as they were called, had begun in 1749 and was expected to be completed by 1753.

The New Barracks were occupied by the soldiers of the *Compagnies franches* while the artillerymen lived in the guardrooms at the top of the St. John and St. Louis gates. After 1755, the New Barracks also had to house soldiers from the *troupes de terre* (regular army) when some of their battalions set up winter quarters in the city of Québec. Except for the period 1753-55, billet lodging remained necessary in Québec, since there were never enough barracks to house all the soldiers who passed through the city, either arriving from France or returning to winter quarters. Essentially, the barracks were intended to house unmarried soldiers. Officers of the *Compagnies franches* lived in the vicinity of the Château Saint-Louis, where their properties were located. Non-commissioned officers who were married lived in the city as well, no doubt because the barracks lacked suitable accommodations. It was not unheard of for married couples to live in the barracks, but such cases appear to have been rare. In 1758 the drum major Julien LeComte lived in the Dauphine Barracks with his wife. In September of that same year, the priest of Notre-Dame de Québec officiated at the burial of an unidentified child who had been brought to the church from the barracks. Obviously, then, families occasionally lived in the barracks.

By its decision to quarter the members of the Québec garrison in barracks, the government reduced opportunities for contact between ordinary soldiers and civilians living in the city, thereby inhibiting friendly exchanges between them. The policy of barracking may thus have played a role in limiting the number of marriages among soldiers stationed in Québec, during the period 1752-56 in particular. Privates who married were usually required to resign from the forces, and thus tended to wait until their term of service was up. In Canada, however, where families were needed to increase the size of the population, soldiers were allowed to marry after serving for three years. In the period 1748-59 there do not appear to have been many marriages among members of the military in Québec. The marriage rate was much higher, however, among non-commissioned officers and artillerymen, who did not have to live in barracks, than among ordinary soldiers of the *Compagnies franches*. Apparently, the higher salaries and more prestigious positions commanded by the non-commissioned officers and artillerymen made them more attractive marriage candidates in the eyes of the widows and daughters of the city's residents.

For the soldiers stationed in Québec, marriage was usually not financially attractive unless it involved a widow with assets to share from a previous marriage. Dowries, when they existed at all, were extremely meager. Another factor in the limited number of marriages in Québec between 1748 and 1759, particularly during the period 1752-56, was the almost total reconstitution of the troops in 1750. In addition to completing at least three years of service before they could marry, the outbreak of hostilities between the French and English in 1755 made it impossible for soldiers to obtain permission to quit the army to get married. As well, between 1753 and 1755 Governor Duquesne was involved in organizing expeditions to the Ohio river and in constant need of men. He was consequently not inclined to be too receptive to requests for early retirement by soldiers wishing to marry. The combined effect of all these factors explains why the marriage rate among members of the military establishment declined during the period 1748-59 and why there were so few married soldiers living in barracks.

We know very little about how the interiors of the barracks were arranged, how they were furnished or how comfortable they were. Military regulations stipulated that each bedroom had to have as many beds (four feet by six feet) as space permitted, plus one table and two chairs. In addition, each bedroom had a fireplace or stove, chests where soldiers could put away their bayonets and swords, and bars and hooks attached to the walls on which they could hang their clothes and utensils. Soldiers slept two to a bed and prepared their meals in the same room. The Military Code attempted to foster a modicum of cleanliness by requiring the soldiers to sweep their rooms every day. Apparently, there were some inconsistencies in the degree of enthusiasm and diligence with which the men in the Québec garrison carried out this requirement. At least, this is what Governor Duquesne seemed to imply by his remark in 1754 that the barracks were more suitable for storing merchandise than for housing soldiers. The barracks must have appeared rather uninviting to the men and inspired a number of escapades on their part. Although barrack-living had been instituted to meet the increased need for discipline, it was evidently not the answer to every problem. Indeed, there were many instances of men staying out all night. Furthermore, according to some of the testimony given at various legal proceedings in Québec, civilians found it fairly easy to enter the area of the New Barracks, in particular, without being detected, despite the fact that it was surrounded by a sentry wall. If civilians could get in, of course, the soldiers could get out.

The men prepared their meals in groups of seven, on the stove or in the fireplace in their barracks. Since they used common cauldrons and plates for cooking and eating, they probably took turns preparing dishes that they were able to make from their daily ration of a pound and a half of bread, a quarter of a pound of pork, and a quarter of a pound of dry peas. On fast days and days of abstinence, fish and vegetables were distributed in place of pork. When possible, soldiers supplemented their rations with fresh vegetables and whatever else they could acquire by hunting or fishing. Occasionally they went to an inn or a tavern where they could get meals that were a little different from their usual stews and barracks fare, and some even purchased meat which they had innkeepers prepare for them. Soldiers also consumed large quantities of wine, brandy and spruce beer, which they could buy at the barracks canteen or in the taverns that proliferated throughout Québec.

Soldiers do not appear to have done any better in the clothing department than they did in the area of furniture, where they were supplied with nothing but the bare essentials. All soldiers were issued uniforms that consisted basically of a blue vest, blue trousers and a pale gray jerkin with blue facing. To complete the outfit, they also received a hemp shirt, blue wool stockings, black leather shoes and a black felt tricorn hat trimmed with an imitation gold braid. Military and civilian dress were similar to each other in terms of cut - they differed only in colour and type of cloth. New uniforms were received from the King every two years and soldiers were expected to pay for any parts that had to be replaced in the interim. When soldiers were on sentry duty during cold or rainy weather, they wore pale gray capes. In winter they adopted the Amerindian fashion of wearing moccasins in place of shoes. The quality of the fabrics used to make the uniforms elicited numerous complaints - the material was often too flimsy to stand up to intens-

1er avril 1755.

Professeurs Sre

CAZERNES. 1755

JE fouffigné Receveur de l'Impofition ordonnée pour l'Entretien des Cazernes de cette Ville, Reconnois avoir reçû de *Louis Parre*

la fomme de *Arrape failles*
conformément au Rolle arrêté pour ladite Année.
A Quebec, le *1er avril 1755.*

8 Taxation receipt for 1755 for the maintenance of the new barracks.
   Archives du Séminaire de Québec, Quebec.

ive use or to the rigours of the Canadian climate. There was dissatisfaction as well about how infrequently the uniforms were replaced. The shortage of new clothing meant that soldiers often had to wear clothes that were torn, wet and dirty. Due to a lack of wells, water was always in short supply in the Québec barracks, and the men were reluctant to waste it on their laundry. When their clothes ripped or split at the seams, they were very often forced to do the mending themselves, to save money or because tailors or tailor's assistants were hard to find. The appearance of the troops was bound to reflect all these limitations.

Soldiers of the Québec garrison were also issued a leather belt, which they usually wore over their jackets. They hung their sword and bayonet from this belt and attached their cartridge pouch and powder horn to it as well. The soldiers used the cartridges and powder to charge their grenade rifles, which were about 1.6 metres long and weighed 4.1 kilograms. In addition to the firearms and knives which were issued to the soldiers, commissioned and non-commissioned officers also had lances. A captain, for example, had a spontoon or half-pike, with which to guide his company, while a sergeant could use his halberd to keep his men in line. As with their uniforms, soldiers were responsible for replacing at their expense any part of their equipment that was lost or worn out. The Military Code prohibited soldiers from wearing their uniforms when they were not performing military duties. When they were not on guard duty or carrying out orders, they were required to leave their weapons in the barracks. The purpose of this provision was not only to encourage the men to take good care of their weapons but to prevent their quarrels from degenerating into duels or murders.

Maintaining proper hygiene in the places where the soldiers had to live was difficult, but of paramount importance. The accumulation of noxious odours below decks in troop transport ships, the transmission of bacteria through the sharing of utensils, the frequent wearing of dirty, wet clothes, and the poor ventilation and dampness of their barracks all contributed to the incubation and rapid spread of disease. The information we have on soldiers admitted to the Hôtel-Dieu Hospital in Québec suggests that illness among the military of the town was caused primarily by diseases contracted on board ship. Indeed, after ships arrived from France in July and August, all the beds in the Hôtel-Dieu Hospital filled up with soldiers. Some years, especially after 1755, it actually became necessary to set up field hospitals and to place the sick in the *Hôpital général* in order to cope with the problems created by the huge numbers of soldiers needing medical care. Injuries suffered on construction jobs ranked second among the causes that sent soldiers to hospital. Despite the fact that medical diagnosis was not very common at the time, it was apparent that, next to infection, the soldiers of the *Compagnies franches* suffered mainly from work-related accidents, battle wounds, nervous disorders and problems brought about by the aging process.

Although civilians far outnumbered soldiers in terms of Québec's general population (about 8000 in 1754), more than half the hospital beds in the city were occupied by soldiers. Moreover, hospital stays were much longer in Canada, averaging about 20 days compared to four to ten days in France. While it is possible to assume from this that soldiers in Canada had more serious illnesses and were provided with less effective treatments, we cannot be sure that this was the case. It may be more accurate to suppose that the soldiers found life in the Hôtel-Dieu Hospital, where they were generally well treated, a good deal more comfortable than life in the barracks. To a number of these lonely newcomers, this hospital must have seemed a haven, a place where they could find refuge from the discipline of military life. In such circumstances, patients tend to prolong their convalescence.

In the period 1748-60 more than 800 soldiers were buried in Québec, not counting the men who fell in battle on the Plains of Abraham or in Sainte-Foy. The men who were buried were not all from the garrison of Québec. In fact, death was far less prevalent among men of the garrison than among the recruits and soldiers of the land forces who were newly arrived from France. The years that saw large numbers of troops disembarked at Québec - 1750, 1756 and 1757 - were the same years that witnessed upsurges in the death rate. While soldiers of the garrison may not have been directly affected by all the deaths, the general impact must have been demoralizing. Soldiers in the *Compagnies franches* in Québec who saw their comrades fall lived in constant fear of epidemics. The risk of disease or even death, combined with the hardships of their environment, greatly diminished any enthusiasm garrison members may have felt for military service.

Military Activities

Since few details are extant regarding the day-to-day activities of the *Compagnies franches de la Marine* garrisoned in Québec, our knowledge in this area remains superficial. According to the Military Code, soldiers were to retire for the night at 8:00 a.m. in winter and at 9:00 a.m. in summer. They were probably expected to rise before 7:00 as that was the time sergeants began barracks inspection. Our only indication of the time reveille was sounded for soldiers in Québec appears in the statement of a soldier quartered in the Dauphine Barracks who was found having breakfast one April morning in a tavern on Saint-Jean street as it was approaching 5 a.m. A statement by another soldier indicates that in February 1752, the men were called to repair to quarters at 7:30 p.m. These examples suggest that the daily military routine practised in Québec adhered to the Military Code. In the summer of 1756, Montcalm's troops were required to work a 13.5-hour workday, from 5:00 a.m. to 8:30 p.m., with two and a half hours off for meals. Generally speaking, reveille was supposed to be sounded at about 4 a.m., 4:30 during the summer semester, and in the evening a drum beat the tattoo sometime between 7:30 and 8:00. In short, a soldier's day was conditioned by the rising and setting of the sun.

Soldiers had to clean their barracks, pass inspection and eat breakfast before they could begin their daily work schedules. Their first duty was to mount guard, to provide some measure of security in the city. To this end they were stationed in the various guardrooms of the city, such as those of the Château Saint-Louis, the New Barracks or the city gates. They were also

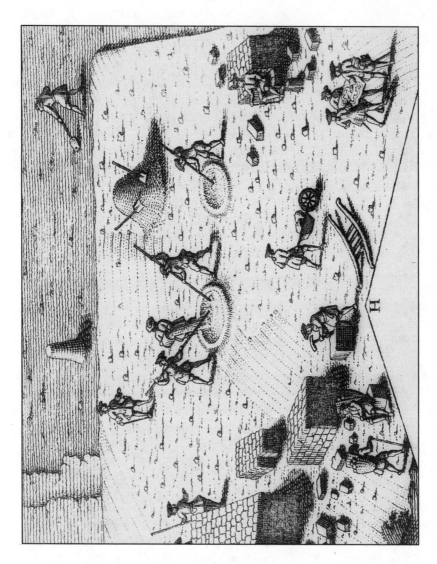

9   Soldiers working on a fortifications construction site.
Bernard Forest de Bélidor, La science des Ingénieurs dans la conduite des travaux de fortifi-
cation et d'architecture civile. Paris, 1729.

posted as sentries in front of certain public buildings such as the Intendant's Palace and the Treasury, and they kept watch on the naval shipyard as well. In addition, soldiers were attached as guards to military prisoners who had to be hospitalized. Regulations stipulated that the squads of soldiers detached for this job had to provide round-the-clock surveillance, with each soldier spending a minimum of four and a maximum of six hours a day on guard duty. With regard to regular sentry duty, the guard was changed every two hours in summer and every hour in winter. In Québec, as in France, shifts began at noon and were not repeated more than once a week unless a soldier volunteered to stand in for one of his fellows.

The garrison of Québec usually assembled to welcome important visitors and to attend the punishment of soldiers sentenced for committing some offence. In addition, soldiers were required to assemble every three months for reviews. They were also expected to participate in military exercises on Sundays and holidays. However, we might well wonder how effective these exercises were. The governors of the time repeatedly complained that officers, having never received the slightest bit of training in France, were ignorant of even the most basic aspects of the Military Code. As a result, undisciplined behaviour was rampant among the men in their command. Although soldiers performed mainly military functions, they had other tasks as well. One of these was to help police find and arrest criminals. When they performed police functions, the soldiers were commanded by a sergeant or corporal and they usually accompanied an officer of the constabulary who, for his part, was primarily in charge of the policemen involved in the operation. The drummers of the garrison had more specific duties. It was their job to sound reveille, taps, the changing of the guard and troop assemblies. Another function was to accompany the bailiffs of the various courts of justice when they held auctions in the public forums and squares of the city of Québec.

Officers of the Québec garrison were conspicuous by their absence. In the summer of 1754, seven companies in the city did not have a single one of their officers present. Non-commissioned officers of the garrison, on the other hand, were a little more engaged. Their role was to provide supervision and maintain discipline. Sergeants visited the barracks, inspected the soldiers' weapons and apparel, conducted roll call and commanded detachments. Corporals had similar duties, but were also required when guard was mounted to inspect the locations to be guarded and to assign sentries to their posts. The artillerymen of Québec, unlike their fellow soldiers in the *Compagnies franches*, did not have to stand guard duty. Rather, they spent their time learning how to handle their weapons, both theoretically and in practice. When artillery had to be used, these men took charge of the guns and cannon, while the soldiers of the *Compagnies franches* and the men of the militia assumed the role of assistants. Sons of *Canadiens* who joined the troops as cadets were considered to be a notch above their fellow soldiers, since they alone could aspire to officer rank. As potential officers waiting for vacancies in commissioned posts, cadets could command the other soldiers when they were sent out in detachments. Their officer-fathers, meanwhile, could turn their attention to clearing land on their seigneuries or to looking after their fur-trade interests.

All soldiers who were fully qualified in a trade or even had a nodding acquaintance with it, could ply it when they had time off from their military duties. They offered their services for hire to middle-class residents of the city of Québec and to inhabitants of the surrounding areas. In 1751, for instance, two soldiers of the Verchères company made a deal with a merchant and former soldier named Pierre Révol, to mine some rock in his yard. The work was to be done for 600 *livres*. Some soldiers worked as gardeners at the Québec seminary, while others worked on behalf of the king as masons, roofers or bakers. Men were also retained by their officers to cut and cure hay on their lands. In Québec, two or three soldiers worked regularly as nurses at the Hôtel-Dieu Hospital, taking care of fellow soldiers who were patients there. Soldiers with no special trade, about half the garrison, found work as day labourers. They were mainly hired to help build the fortifications and New Barracks of Québec, projects that were carried out in the period 1745-57.

These construction projects, undertaken to improve Québec's defences, were in part responsible for the pronounced increase in the number of soldiers sent to Canada in 1750. Colonial authorities viewed the work contributed by the soldiers as an ideal way to alleviate the scarcity and high cost of unskilled labour. Non-commissioned officers earned five to 10 *sols* more for a day's labour than ordinary soldiers, who were paid one *livre*. In 1748 a soldier employed by the King as a baker was paid 370 *livres* a year. Soldiers assigned to police duties were awarded bonuses for each arrest they made. For example, a corporal and four soldiers received six *livres* 10 *sols* for taking sailors from the ship *Le Cerf* to prison in 1750. However, soldiers were paid half the amount of wages that civilians received for the same work. This difference was rather profitable for employers and encouraged them to hire soldiers.

While some of the soldiers worked for wages, many preferred to run their own businesses, and in 1750 colonial authorities were moved to express their disapproval of the fact that a number of sergeants were operating taverns. It is not hard to imagine the pressures that a sergeant could exert to persuade the men in his company to patronize his establishment, although it is just as easy to picture the effects that the consumption of alcohol must have had on discipline. It was probably impossible for sergeants who owned taverns to resist the temptation to put their profits ahead of their respect for the Military Code. Other soldiers became pedlars, buying goods from the merchants of Québec and selling them in the countryside. More than one soldier believed that when it came to starting up a business, the end justified the means. Dominique Ducos *dit* Lesperance bought and sold liquor in Rivière-du-Loup-en-haut in 1757, and the alcohol he handled came into his possession as a result of a robbery at the parish rectory.

Rolling casks for a warehouse keepers, firing guns to celebrate a baby's birth and being paid in liquor, or saving their rations in order to sell them, were some of the ways soldiers could improve lot in life. The fact that men collected wages for work other than soldiering explains how some of them were able to pay their fellow soldiers to fill in for them on guard duty. While purely military activities did not always engage their interest or wholehearted participation, at least according to the authorities, the chance to make money made them more than willing to hire themselves out by the day. In general, the men seemed to appreciate the opportunity to increase their pay, whether it was through wages or other means. Soldiers were paid six *livres*, 15 *sols* a month net in service to the King, and artillerymen received two to four *livres* more than soldiers. However, the amount of pay the men received remained unchanged from 1748 through to 1759, even though prices, as a result of inflation, were on average 20 times higher by the end of this period than they were at the beginning. A dozen eggs, which cost three *sols* in 1751, were worth three *livres* 10 sols in 1759. Consequently, the soldiers had to look elsewhere for the means to obtain what their military pay could not provide. Still, they were fortunate in that their rations, which they received *free* and could barter, were one of the items that went up in value during this period.

Non-commissioned officers were paid double the wages of ordinary soldiers and the salaries of officers were five to 15 times higher than that of their subordinates. The officers knew that even though their pay was higher, it would never make them rich and that if they wanted to improve their life, they had to develop their seigneuries or do a little fur trading. Soldiers were paid every three months during the reviews held by the administrative staff. If soldiers wanted to collect their pay, they had to take part in the reviews. If they were absent due to hospitalization or to participation in a detachment, their pay was kept by the paymaster until they returned to their garrisons. This requirement prevented officers from claiming the wages of soldiers who were deceased or on sessional leave.

It is difficult to assess the overall economic impact of the military presence in Québec or indeed anywhere else in Canada. On their meager pay, soldiers could not spend much on local or imported products, even though they added to their incomes by working outside the service. As a result of the extra money they earned, however, the taverns in the city of Québec made a good living. Soldiers found many ways to increase the size of their paycheque. Some became merchants, selling liquor, linen and other products, while others made a noteworthy contribution to the colony through their labour. At a time when manpower was scarce, soldiers were willing to work for less pay than civilians. For this reason alone, the economic contribution made by the men of the garrison of Québec appears to have been fairly substantial.

Living Habits and Leisure Activities

Patronizing inns and taverns was unquestionably the favorite and probably the most easily accessible leisure activity of the soldiers. Whether it was the *Reine Blanche* on the de la Montagne street or the *Lion d'Or* on Saint-Louis Street, the soldiers of Québec went to inns and taverns whenever they could. On Sundays they went at times when there were no church services and on other days they went whenever they were off duty. During the period 1750-53, when the city of Québec had less than 8000 inhabitants, at least 81 Québeckers operated inns or taverns. Moreover, 11 establishments were owned by some non-commissioned officers and former soldiers. It seems that the military clientele had only one problem - how to choose which tavern or inn to frequent. The appetite the soldiers had for such establishments no doubt prompted them to make certain career choices.

The taverns where soldiers went to eat, drink and talk were very often the scene of arguments among the men. In 1751, following a quarrel that started in an inn on des Remparts Street owned by François Morar *dit* la Forme, the gunner Jean Corollaire fought a duel with a fellow soldier. The two men escaped punishment by running away. Frequenting bars also gave the men an opportunity to meet women, to dance, and to play cards, dice and billiards. In the evenings at *Vadeboncoeur*, Marguerite Brusseau's place on Saint-François Street, the soldiers jumped and danced so hard the rafters shook. Evidently, dancing and games of chance were available even to the members of the military who were never invited to governors' balls or to social functions presided over by Intendant Bigot and the officers.

Athletic activities for soldiers were rather limited. Organized sports were unknown in New France at that time, and hunting, fishing and swimming were looked upon by the men as activities performed for specific purposes, such as washing themselves or supplementing their diets, which occasionally left something to be desired. In winter the soldiers went on sleigh rides in the countryside around Québec. While soldiers commonly sought to take their minds off the boredom and hardships of life in the colony by drinking themselves into a stupor or by puffing on their pipes (they received a pound of tobacco every month), they were also able to look forward to the more satisfying relief offered by sessional leave. Every year until 1754, a certain number of soldiers were permitted to return to France for the winter semester. The reason for granting these leaves of absence was to give the men an opportunity to settle their family problems and, sometimes, to do some recruiting. However, the soldiers often saw this holiday as an ideal occasion for disentangling themselves from their military commitments.

Soldiers did not always wait until they obtained sessional leave to quit the service. Indeed, desertion was the most frequent offence committed among the soldiers of New France. There were many reasons why men deserted, but the most common seem to have been boredom, debts and the desire to escape punishment. It was harder for a soldier in the garrison of Québec to desert than for a soldier detached to a post in the West, who had an easier time eluding his pursuers as well as a wider choice of destinations. Soldiers who deserted could return to France, usually by making their way to the Gaspé and boarding a fishing vessel, or they could find refuge in the English colonies or among the Amerindians. The penalty for desertion was death but, given the circumstances, the sentence very often had to be imposed by default. If soldiers deserted in a group and were captured, the offence still called for capital punishment.

To avoid the spilling of too much blood the men were instructed to draw lots, the loser was executed and the others were sentenced to hard labour.

Other, less serious acts of insubordination included a refusal to obey orders and a failure to show proper respect for an officer. Since the minutes of court-martial proceedings describing acts of insubordination no longer exist, it is difficult to assess accurately the kind or extent of delinquency among the soldiers of the *Compagnies franches*. The observations offered by government officials were more in the nature of general comments deploring the evils of drink and lack of discipline that were so widespread among the men. Men who failed to show respect for their officers often escaped punishment completely by changing companies. The independence of the companies in the *Compagnies franches* made this type of transfer possible. Despite all the remarks describing how undisciplined the men were, the fact that there was never a mutiny among them suggests that the soldiers of the *Compagnies franches* did have some respect for the established order.

According to the records of the Superior Council and of the Provost's office of Québec, where cases involving soldiers and civilians were tried, the most frequently committed crime among members of the military establishment in Québec, next to desertion and insubordination, was robbery. In most instances, the perpetrators broke into government buildings or the premises of private individuals. In 1758 Roch Bailly, a drummer in the Columbière company, took a dozen napkins from the dining hall of the Château Saint-Louis. He was in a state of inebriation at the time he committed the theft, having visited several bars after coming off guard duty. Thefts involving money were rather rare, since in Canada metal coins were scarce and paper money was not generally accepted. However, some soldiers took advantage of the monetary system then in effect in Canada by introducing counterfeit money. They turned their three-*livres* notes into 30-*livres* notes, and disposed of them in the shops of merchants who did not always pay close attention to the money customers gave them.

Again according to the records of the Superior Council and the Provost's office, in the period 1748-59 the soldiers of Québec committed no murders or sexual crimes such as rape or seduction. In the two or three duels witnessed in Québec during this time, only one of the participants died of his wounds. While deserters generally faced the death sentence, robbers and forgers were less severely punished. Except during the siege of Québec in the summer of 1759, when robbers were executed the day they committed their crime, the usual penalties imposed on offenders were hard labour, flogging, branding with an iron, the wooden horse or banishment. Imprisonment was not a common form of punishment at that time. Soldiers spent time in prison while their trials were in progress or were incarcerated for periods of one month following an act of insubordination. In Québec and elsewhere in Canada, criminal activity in the military population tended to mushroom after 1755. With the arrival of new recruits and members of the regular army (*troupes de terre*) the number of soldiers in the colony increased appreciably, and it was probably this factor that was responsible for the rising incidence of delinquent behaviour. The rather appalling economic conditions experienced both in New France and in its capital during this period occasionally forced soldiers to resort to means that were not always strictly legal, though perhaps not entirely illegitimate, to improve their standard of living.

Conclusion

During his voyage to Canada in 1749, the Swedish scientist Pehr Kalm formed the perception that soldiers in the colony had a fairly easy life. He saw them as well-clothed, well-fed, well-paid men who enjoyed excellent health and benefits that could not be found anywhere else. The attractive portrait painted by Kalm has been altered somewhat by the profile of the soldiers' lives that has been drawn on these pages. Young Frenchmen took up careers as soldiers not because they wanted to but because they had no choice. They had to contend with an inhospitable climate and obey orders from colonial officers who were alien to them. The soldiers made a valuable economic contribution both as workers and as consumers. They increased the labour force and stimulated business in the city of Québec. But in difficult times like those experienced in Québec in the years following 1755, when demand very often exceeded supply, the soldiers were also involuntary agents of inflation. While they certainly did defend the ramparts of Québec, their priority was not to advance the colonial experiment but to ensure their own survival. Their motives and their inexperience thus limited the aid that they were able to bring to the country. Fortunately, the members of Canada's militia brought more passion to the task of protecting their corner of the world, and it was to these men that the country ultimately looked for its defence.

Barracks-quartering, first introduced to meet the housing needs of the soldiers of the Québec garrison, was also intended to establish stricter discipline among the men, a difficult objective to achieve. The barracks system limited the mobility of the soldiers, thereby restricting civilian access to military workers. In this sense, quartering the men in barracks was not necessarily in the best interests of civilians. More importantly, it deprived the men of ways to increase their incomes. In the eyes of the soldiers, whose furniture and other amenities in the barracks were limited to the bare essentials, the move to their new habitat deprived them of creature comforts. When living conditions became unbearable, the men could vent their frustration by getting drunk or indulging in acts of insubordination. More often, however, violations of the Military Code were the only way soldiers had of expressing themselves. Their voices, unfortunately, were sometimes ignored in contemporary travellers' accounts.

Bibliographic Note

This booklet summarizes the work, *Soldat à Québec, 1748-1759*, published in 1977 as No. 242 in the Manuscript Report Series, Parks Services, Environment Canada. A summary of this work appeared in the *Revue d'histoire de l'Amérique française* in March 1979. The reader may find in the unpublished work all the critical analysis, references and notes on which this text is based.

For further information on soldiers and military life in New France, please see the works listed below.

Chartrand, René
The French Soldier in Colonial America. Museum Restoration Service, Ottawa, 1984.

Eccles, W.J.
"The Social, Economic and Political Significance of the Military Establishment in New France," *Canadian Historical Review*, Vol. 52, No. 1 (March 1971).

Greer, Alan
"The Soldiers of Isle Royale, 1720-1745," *History and Archaeology*, Vol. 28, Parks Canada, 1979, Ottawa.

Lanctôt, Gustave
"Les troupes de la Nouvelle-France," *Canadian Historical Review*, Vol. 16, No. 2 (June 1935).

Leclerc, Jean
Le Marquis de Denonville gouverneur de la Nouvelle-France, 1685-1689. Fides, Montréal, 1976. Chapter 4 is devoted to the installation of the marine troops in Canada.

Malchelosse, G.
"Milice et Troupes de la Marine en Nouvelle-France 1669-1760," *Cahier des Dix*, Vol. 14, 1949.
—. *Le régiment de Carignan*. G. Ducharme, Montréal, 1925.

Sulte, Benjamin
"L'organisation militaire du Canada 1636-1648," *Mémoires de la Société Royale du Canada*, May 1986.

—. "Troupes du Canada 1670-1687," *Mémoires de la Société Royale du Canada*, May 1920.

Stanley, G.F.C.
Nos soldats. L'histoire militaire du Canada de 1604 à nos jours. Editions de l'Homme, Montréal, 1980.